QUOTES TO LIVE BY

Words That INSPIRE Those Who INSPIRE US

Aadamsmedia

Avon, Massachusetts

Published by
Adams Media, a division of F+W Media, Inc.
57 Littlefield Street, Avon, MA 02322. U.S.A.
www.adamsmedia.com

ISBN 10: 1-4405-6088-9
ISBN 13: 978-1-4405-6088-0
eISBN 10: 1-4405-6089-7
eISBN 13: 978-1-4405-6089-7

Printed in the United States of America.

10 9 8 7 6 5 4 3 2 1

This book is available at quantity discounts for bulk purchases.
For information, please call 1-800-289-0963.

Contents

"Life itself is a quotation."

—Jorge Luis Borges

Introduction

 Every man is a quotation from all his ancestors."

—*Ralph Waldo Emerson*, essayist, lecturer, poet

The wisdom of our predecessors is preserved in their unforget-table words. The successful, the innovative, the brilliant, and the bold are forever alive in witticisms and proverbs we can't seem to shake.

The most important ones, though, may be the words that empowered our own heroes. An ancient proverb may have changed an artist's perspective forever. A mentor's instructions may have guided an activist's philosophy. An anonymous letter may have touched a leader's heart forever.

People we respect and admire have used all of the quota-tions in this collection through speeches, lectures, interviews, letters, and books of their own. They have relied on these words of wisdom to send off graduating classes, to honor others' suc-cesses, and to empower nations. Some of the quotations have been cornerstones to some of the world's most famous speech-es, well-worn and powerful in their own right; others may have had less weight when first mentioned, but reflect something deeper, more meaningful in retrospect.

Whatever the case, whatever the context, these 142 quota-tions made a difference in the lives of the most successful, inspir-ing people in the world—and they can change yours, too.

Be Courageous

 I learned that courage was not the absence of fear, but the triumph over it. The brave man is not he who does not feel afraid, but he who conquers that fear."

—*Nelson Mandela,* President of South Africa, activist

SHERYL SANDBERG CHIEF OPERATING OFFICER OF FACEBOOK AND ITS FIRST FEMALE BOARD MEMBER

 What would you do if you weren't afraid?"

—*Spencer Johnson,* bestselling author of *Who Moved My Cheese?*

Carry your courage in an easily accessible place, the way you do your cellphone or your wallet. Courage is the ultimate career move."

—*Anna Quindlen,* bestselling author and journalist

Defeat is never fatal. Victory is never final. It's courage that counts."

—*Winston Churchill,* politician, statesman

There were so many things they said women couldn't do and blacks couldn't do. Every defeat to me was a challenge."

—*Marian Wright Edelman,* president and founder of Children's Defense Fund

All great and honorable actions are accompanied with great difficulties, and both must be enterprised and overcome with answerable courage."

—*William Bradford,* second governor of Plymouth Colony and author of *Of Plymouth Plantation*

I know we're going to die. But some of us are going to do something about it."

—*Tom Burnett,* passenger on hijacked United Airlines Flight 93, which crashed in a field near Shanksville, Pennsylvania on September 11, 2001

If I'm ever to reach any understanding of myself and the things around me, I must learn to stand alone."

—*Henrik Ibsen,* from his play, *A Doll's House*

There are some things you learn best in calm, some in storm."

—*Willa Cather,* Pulitzer Prize–winning novelist, quoted as an epigraph to Hannah's novel *Home Front*

WALTER ISAACSON CELEBRATED BIOGRAPHER

 Don't be afraid,
you can do it."

—*Steve Jobs,* co-founder of Apple, Inc.

TED KENNEDY UNITED STATES SENATOR, IN HIS EULOGY FOR ROBERT F. KENNEDY

 I am a part of all that I have
met . . .
To [Tho] much is taken, much
abides . . .
That which we are, we are;
One equal temper of heroic
hearts . . .
Strong in will
To strive, to seek, to find, and
not to yield."

—*Alfred Lord Tennyson,* from his poem,
"Ulysses"

You do not determine a man's greatness by his talent or wealth, as the world does, but rather by what it takes to discourage him."

—*Jerry Falwell,* pastor

Failure seldom stops you. What stops you is the fear of failure."

—*Jack Lemmon,* actor

PARAG KHANNA INTERNATIONAL RELATIONS EXPERT, GEOPOLITICAL ADVISOR, AUTHOR

 What doesn't kill me makes me stronger."

—*Arthur Schopenhauer,* philosopher

Only those who will risk going too far can possibly find out how far one can go."

—*T. S. Eliot,* poet, playwright, publisher

Serve Humanity

 The best way to find yourself is to lose yourself in the service of others."

—*Mahatma Gandhi,* Indian nationalist leader, pioneer of non-violent civil disobedience

The central fact is that man is fundamentally a moral being, that the light we have is imperfect does not matter so long as we are always trying to improve it . . . ”

—*Gladstone Murray,* Canadian politician

Tear down that mirror. Tear down that mirror that makes you always look at yourself. Tear down that mirror and you will be able to look beyond and you will see the millions and millions of people that need your help."

—*Sargent Shriver,* Director of the Peace Corps, Director of the Office of Economic Opportunity, United States Ambassador to France

Our problems are man-made; therefore, they can be solved by man."

—*John F. Kennedy,* President of the United States

Not everybody can be famous. But everybody can be great, because greatness is determined by service."

—*Martin Luther King, Jr.,* leader of the civil rights movement, Nobel Peace Prize winner

JEAN-MARIE GUSTAVE LE CLÉZIO AUTHOR, WINNER OF
THE NOBEL PRIZE IN LITERATURE

 How is it possible on the
one hand, for example, to
behave as if nothing on earth
were more important than
literature, and on the other
fail to see that wherever one
looks, people are struggling
against hunger and will
necessarily consider that the
most important thing is what
they earn at the end of the
month? Because this is where

he (the writer) is confronted with a new paradox: while all he wanted was to write for those who are hungry, he now discovers that it is only those who have plenty to eat who have the leisure to take notice of his existence."

—*Stig Dagerman,* author

Three things in human life are important. The first is to be kind. The second is to be kind. And the third is to be kind."

—*Henry James,* author

Men must be taught as if you taught them not, And things unknown proposed as things forgot."

—*Alexander Pope,* poet

WILL SMITH ACTOR

 If you gonna be here, then there's a necessity to make a difference."

—*His grandmother*

Public business, my son, must always be done by somebody. It will be done by somebody or another. If wise men decline it, others will not; if honest men refuse it, others will not."

—*John Adams,* President of the United States

Once in a lifetime the longed-for tidal wave of justice can rise up, and hope and history rhyme."

—*Seamus Heaney,* poet, playwright, and winner of the Nobel Prize in literature

Lead Boldly

 Stand upright, speak thy thoughts, declare The truth thou hast, that all may share; Be bold, proclaim it everywhere: They only live who dare."

—*Voltaire*, writer, historian, philosopher

Always investigate, always argue, always reason."

—*Shantarakshita,* eighth-century Indian Buddhist Brahmin, abbot of Nalanda University

If you want to serve an age, betray it."

—*Brendan Kennelly*, poet, novelist

I will not equivocate, I will not excuse."

—*William Lloyd Garrison*, abolitionist, journalist, social reformer

From those to whom much is given, much is expected."

—*Mary Maxwell Gates,* his mother, on board of regents for University of Washington, first female president of King's County United Way, first woman to chair national United Way executive committee

There are three types of people in this world: there are those that make it happen; there are those that watch it happen; and then there are those that woke up one day and say 'What the heck happened?' So which one are you?"

—*Ray Akins,* his grandfather, champion high school football coach

HENRY KISSINGER UNITED STATES NATIONAL SECURITY ADVISOR, UNITED STATES SECRETARY OF STATE, WINNER OF THE NOBEL PEACE PRIZE

 If you don't strive for the best, you will never make it."

—*Gerald Ford,* President of the United States

Be bold, Mr. President. We may make mistakes, but we are ready to experiment."

—An unnamed constituent in a letter to Carter

DENZEL WASHINGTON ACTOR

 There is no passion to be found playing small—in settling for a life that's less than the one you're capable of living."

—*Nelson Mandela,* President of South Africa, activist

JILL ABRAMSON JOURNALIST, FIRST FEMALE EXECUTIVE EDITOR
OF *THE NEW YORK TIMES*

 Oh, you'd never
leave the *[Wall
Street] Journal.*"

—*Maureen Dowd,* journalist, just before
Abramson first applied for a job at *The New
York Times*

NANCY PELOSI MINORITY LEADER OF THE UNITED STATES HOUSE OF REPRESENTATIVES, FIRST FEMALE SPEAKER OF THE UNITED STATES HOUSE OF REPRESENTATIVES

 Mother, get a life."

—*Alexandra Pelosi,* her daughter, journalist, filmmaker, when Nancy asked if Alexandra minded if Nancy ran for Congress

STEVE FORBES EDITOR-IN-CHIEF OF *FORBES MAGAZINE,* PRESIDENT AND CEO OF FORBES, INC.

 # I am going to remain independent."

—*B. C. Forbes,* founder of *Forbes Magazine,* when he turned down an offer to sell his company

SAUL PERLMUTTER ASTROPHYSICIST, WINNER OF THE NOBEL PRIZE IN PHYSICS, WHO ADDED HIS OWN VARIANT, "WITH OUR WORK EXPLORING THE UNIVERSE, WE FEEL WHAT IT IS TO BE HUMAN."

 # With his work, as with a glove, a man feels the universe."

—*Tomas Tranströmer,* winner of the Nobel Prize in literature

A dreamer is one who can only find his way by moonlight, and his punishment is that he sees the dawn before the rest of the world."

—*Oscar Wilde,* author, playwright

ROY O. DISNEY CO-FOUNDER AND FIRST CEO OF THE WALT DISNEY COMPANY

 # Let's not throw away the good stuff."

—*Walt Disney,* co-founder of the Walt Disney Company, upon seeing sketches artists threw out believing they weren't strong enough

 **Watch me."**

—*Army Staff Sergeant Amy Krueger,*
when she enlisted after 9/11 and her mother
said she couldn't take on Osama bin Laden
alone

If you want to build a flotilla of ships, you don't sit around talking about carpentry. No, you need to set people's souls ablaze with visions of exploring distant shores."

—*Antoine de Saint-Exupéry,* novelist, poet, aviator

Work Hard and Rise to Life's Challenges

 The way I see it, if you want the rainbow, you gotta put up with the rain."

—*Dolly Parton,* singer-songwriter, actress

Honesty is the best policy."

—*Miguel de Cervantes,* novelist

 # Liars prosper."

—*Anonymous*

Every bump is a bounce."

—*Robert Kraft,* Chairman and CEO of the Kraft Group

Beyond mountains there are mountains."

—*Haitian proverb*

Nothing that is worth doing can be achieved in our lifetime; therefore we must be saved by hope. Nothing which is true or beautiful or good makes complete sense in any immediate context of history, therefore we must be saved by faith. Nothing we do, however virtuous, can be accomplished alone; therefore we must be saved by love."

—*Reinhold Niebuhr,* theologian

It is better to
light one candle
than to curse the
darkness."

—*Chinese proverb*

I never have a holiday. On Monday towards noon I lift up my head, and breathe for about an hour; after that the wicket shuts again and I am in my prison cell for seven days."

—*Charles Augustin Sainte-Beuve,* literary critic

There needs to be time for efficient data collection and time for inefficient contemplation, time to operate the machine and time to sit idly in the garden."

—*Nicholas Carr,* author, Pulitzer Prize finalist

You don't do things right once in a while. You do them right all the time."

—*Vince Lombardi,* head coach of the Green Bay Packers

I'm no genius. I'm smart in spots but I stay around those spots."

—*Thomas J. Watson, Sr.,* chairman and CEO of IBM

Even in our sleep, pain which
cannot forget
falls drop by drop upon the
heart,
until, in our own despair,
against our will,
comes wisdom through the
awful grace of God."

—*Aeschylus,* Greek playwright, quoted by
Kennedy during his eulogy of Martin Luther
King, Jr.

AL GORE VICE PRESIDENT OF THE UNITED STATES, ON TAKING ACTION

 When you pray, move your feet."

—*African proverb*

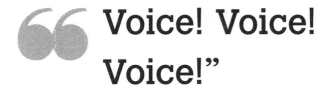 **Voice! Voice! Voice!"**

—*Nora Ephron,* her criticism given upon reading a piece of Hanks's writing

MICHAEL CHABON PULITZER PRIZE–WINNING AUTHOR, ON GROWING UP DIFFERENT AND ACCEPTING THOSE DIFFERENCES

 From childhood's hour I have not been
As others were—I have not seen
As others saw—I could not bring
My passions from a common spring."

—*Edgar Allan Poe,* author, poet, editor

Comedy's a funny game, it's not a job, it's a vocation— you never stop."

—*Eric Sykes,* comedian

[The] only way to do great work is to love what you do."

—*Steve Jobs,* co-founder of Apple, Inc.

The person who wants to make it has to sweat! There are no shortcuts. And you've got to have the guts to be hated—that's the hard part. It's only the work that truly satisfies. I think I've known this all my life. No one could ever share my drive or visions. No one has ever understood the sweetness of my job at the end of a good day's work."

—*Bette Davis,* actress

Dream Big

 Every great dream begins with a dreamer. Always remember, you have within you the strength, the patience, and the passion to reach for the stars to change the world."

—*Harriet Tubman*, abolitionist, humanitarian

What we achieve inwardly will change outer reality."

—*Plutarch,* Greek philosopher

Fiction reveals the truth that reality obscures."

—*Jessamyn West,* author

[The humanity of people is] not so wild a dream as those who profit by delaying it would have us believe."

—Unknown

This wall will fall. Belief will become reality."

—Unknown graffiti artist who painted the words on the Berlin Wall

MARTIN LUTHER KING, JR. LEADER OF THE CIVIL RIGHTS MOVEMENT, NOBEL PEACE PRIZE WINNER

 Free at last! Free at last! Thank God Almighty we are free at last!"

—*Spiritual*

I've got two months, but my life's dream was to learn calculus, and Khan Academy has given [me] that. And I look forward to spending the last two months of my life learning it."

—Unnamed viewer

My object in living is to unite

My avocation and my vocation

As my two eyes make one in sight."

—*Robert Frost,* poet

When I go from hence, let this be my parting word, that what I have seen is unsurpassable."

—*Rabindranath Tagore*, poet, composer, essayist, playwright, painter, first non-European winner of the Nobel Prize in literature

Everything you can imagine is real."

—*Pablo Picasso,* painter, sculptor

If we'd known we were going to be The Beatles we'd have tried harder."

—*George Harrison,* Beatles's lead guitarist

Chiisaku matomanna yo." (Translated literally from Japanese: "Don't reduce yourself into something small." Translated more figuratively: "Think big!")

—*Honjo,* a character in the Japanese cartoon *Chance*

Some men see things as they are and say why. I dream things that never were and say why not."

—*Robert F. Kennedy,* United States Senator, United States Attorney General

RAY BRADBURY AWARD-WINNING AUTHOR, PIONEER OF
SCIENCE FICTION, FANTASY, HORROR, AND MYSTERY FICTION

 We have art so that we do not die of reality. Reality is too much with us."

—*Friedrich Nietzsche*, philosopher

We are out in a country that has no language, no laws. Whatever we do together is pure invention. The maps they gave us are out of date by years."

—*Adrienne Rich,* poet, essayist, on the possibilities and future of art

Challenge Expectations

" I'm not in this world to live up to your expectations and you're not in this world to live up to mine."

—*Bruce Lee,* actor, martial arts instructor

Every significant invention must be startling, unexpected, and must come into a world that is not prepared for it. If the world were prepared for it, it would not be much of an invention."

—*Edwin H. Land,* inventor of the Polaroid camera and co-founder of the Polaroid Corporation

[Have a] healthy disregard for the impossible."

—*Slogan for Leaderscape,* a University of Michigan summer leadership course which Page attended

STEVEN CHU NOBEL PRIZE–WINNING PHYSICIST AND UNITED
STATES SECRETARY OF ENERGY

 I skate to where
the puck is going
to be, not where
it's been."

—*Wayne Gretzky,* professional ice hockey
player and member of the Hockey Hall of
Fame

CLARENCE DARROW LAWYER, FOUNDING MEMBER OF THE ACLU, DEFENSE ATTORNEY FOR LEOPOLD AND LOEB, AND THE SCOPES "MONKEY" TRIAL

 So I be written in the Book of Love,
I do not care about that Book above.
Erase my name or write it as you will,
So I be written in the Book of Love."

—*Omar Khayyám,* poet, philosopher, mathematician, astronomer

NELSON MANDELA PRESIDENT OF SOUTH AFRICA, DURING HIS TRIAL, ON THE DECISION TO DEPART FROM THE AFRICAN NATIONAL CONGRESS'S PEACEFUL WORK AGAINST APARTHEID, EXPRESSING THE EXTENT TO WHICH ONE MAY BE PUSHED TO DEFEAT VIOLENT OPPRESSORS

 We had to overcome our weakness for mankind . . . that deep-rooted conviction of ours that no victor ever pays, whereas any mutilation of mankind is irrevocable."

—*Albert Camus,* author, journalist, philosopher

I am a true adorer of life, and if I can't reach as high as the face of it, I plant my kiss somewhere lower down. Those who understand will require no further explanation."

—*Saul Bellow,* author, winner of the Pulitzer Prize, the Nobel Prize in literature, and the National Medal of the Arts

A genius can
do readily what
nobody else can
do at all."

—*Herbert Spencer,* philosopher

RAY BRADBURY AWARD-WINNING AUTHOR, PIONEER OF
SCIENCE FICTION, FANTASY, HORROR, AND MYSTERY FICTION

 If they give you
ruled paper, write
the other way."

—*Juan Ramón Jiménez,* poet, winner of the
Nobel Prize in literature

Lawyers, I suppose, were children once."

—*Charles Lamb,* essayist, offering a challenging perspective

I realized my mission in life was to learn more, not earn more."

—*Surya Das,* Tibetan Buddhist lama

 # Nothing is inevitable."

—*Samuel J. Palmisano,* her predecessor as CEO of IBM

Ever tried. Ever failed. No matter. Try again. Fail again. Fail better."

—*Samuel Beckett,* playwright, novelist, winner of the Nobel Prize in literature

Expand Your Worldview

 A man who views the world the same at fifty as he did at twenty has wasted thirty years of his life."

—*Muhammad Ali,* professional boxer, philanthropist, activist

Liberty is never being too sure you're right."

—*Learned Hand,* judge, philosopher

If we cannot now end
our differences, at least
we can help make the
world safe for diversity."

—*John F. Kennedy,* President of the United States

There is still, brothers, so much to do."

—*César Vallejo,* poet

ELIZABETH GURLEY FLYNN LABOR LEADER, ACTIVIST, FEMINIST, FOUNDING MEMBER OF THE ACLU

 This country with its institutions belongs to the people who inhabit it."

—*Abraham Lincoln,* President of the United States

BARBARA JORDAN CIVIL RIGHTS LEADER, FIRST AFRICAN AMERICAN TEXAS STATE SENATOR, FIRST SOUTHERN AFRICAN AMERICAN FEMALE UNITED STATES REPRESENTATIVE, HONORED WITH THE PRESIDENTIAL MEDAL OF FREEDOM

 Let us restore to social intercourse that harmony and that affection without which liberty and even life are but dreary things."

—*Thomas Jefferson,* President of the United States

[The] strength of the Wolf is in the pack."

—*Rudyard Kipling*, author

If you are going to grow into a human being, you are going to need some values."

—*Ann Dunham,* his mother, anthropologist

MITCH DANIELS GOVERNOR OF INDIANA, PRESIDENT OF
PURDUE UNIVERSITY

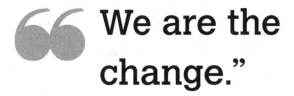 We are the
change."

—*Ronald Reagan,* President of the United
States

We must not see any person as an abstraction. Instead, we must see in every person a universe with its own secrets, with its own treasures, with its own sources of anguish, and with some measure of triumph."

—*Elie Wiesel,* author, Nobel Peace Prize winner, Holocaust survivor

The vote is a power, a weapon of offense and defense, a prayer. Understand what it means and what it can do for your country."

—*Carrie Chapman Catt,* women's suffrage leader, president of the National American Woman Suffrage Association, founder of League of Women Voters and International Alliance of Women

Kinship among nations is not determined in such measurements as proximity, size and age. Rather, we should turn to those inner things—call them what you will—I mean those intangibles that are the real treasures free men possess."

—*Dwight D. Eisenhower,* President of the United States

The real point is that you cannot harbor malice toward others and then cry foul when someone displays intolerance against you. Prejudice tolerated is intolerance encouraged. Rise up in righteousness when you witness the words and deeds of hate, but only if you are willing to rise up against them all, including your own."

—*Harvey Fierstein,* actor, playwright

Freedom has many difficulties and democracy is not perfect. But we have never had to put a wall up to keep our people in."

—*John F. Kennedy,* President of the United States

JACQUELINE NOVOGRATZ FOUNDER AND CEO OF
THE NON-PROFIT VENTURE CAPITAL FIRM ACUMEN FUND, ON
UNDERSTANDING THE EFFECTS OF GLOBAL POVERTY

Better immersion than to live untouched."

—*Tillie Olsen,* author

Listen

You do not need to leave your room. Remain sitting at your table and listen. Do not even listen, simply wait, be quiet, still and solitary. The world will freely offer itself to you to be unmasked, it has no choice, it will roll in ecstasy at your feet."

—*Franz Kafka,* author

Emotion is the chief source of becoming conscious. There can be no transforming of lightness into dark, of apathy into movement without emotion."

—*Carl Jung,* psychologist, psychiatrist

Mind is an excellent servant but a terrible master."

—*Adage*

What is a man profited, if he shall gain the whole world, and lose his own soul?"

—*Matthew 16:26*

GERALDINE FERRARO UNITED STATES REPRESENTATIVE, FIRST FEMALE VICE PRESIDENTIAL CANDIDATE FOR A MAJOR PARTY, ATTORNEY

 Occasionally in life there are moments which cannot be completely explained by words. Their meaning can only be articulated by the inaudible language of the heart."

—*Martin Luther King, Jr.*, leader of the civil rights movement, Nobel Peace Prize winner

Man is only half himself, the other half is his expression."

—*Ralph Waldo Emerson,* essayist, lecturer, poet

The present contains nothing more than the past. And what is found in the effect was already in the cause."

—*Henri Bergson,* philosopher

Surely whoever speaks to me in the right voice, him or her I shall follow.
As the water follows the moon, silently, with fluid steps anywhere around the globe."

—*Walt Whitman,* poet

DAVID MCCULLOUGH AUTHOR, HISTORIAN, PULITZER PRIZE WINNER, WINNER OF THE NATIONAL BOOK AWARD

 We can never tell what is in store for us."

—*Harry Truman,* President of the United States

Every blade of grass has its Angel that bends over it and whispers, 'Grow, grow.'"

—*The Talmud*

Lovers don't finally meet somewhere. They're in each other all along."

—*Rumi,* poet, jurist, theologian, mystic

ANDY GRIFFITH ACTOR, WHILE SPEAKING OF HIS FRIENDSHIP WITH LINDSEY AND THEIR ABILITY TO SAY THIS TO EACH OTHER OFTEN IN THEIR OLD AGE

 I love you."

—*George Lindsey,* actor best known for his role as "Goober Pyle"

MAE JEMISON PHYSICIAN, NASA ASTRONAUT, FIRST BLACK WOMAN IN SPACE

 The most beautiful thing we can experience is the mysterious. It is the source of all true art and science."

—*Albert Einstein,* physicist

STANLEY MCCHRYSTAL UNITED STATES ARMY GENERAL, ON THE IMPORTANCE OF HAVING SUCH FRIENDSHIPS IN HIS MILITARY CAREER AND BEYOND

 I knew if I ever got in a tight spot, that you would come, if alive."

—*William Tecumseh Sherman,* Union Army General, to then-Union General and future-United States President Ulysses S. Grant

Treat your audience like poets and geniuses, and that's how they'll behave."

—*Del Close,* actor, improviser, writer, and teacher

You might not know it, but this is your best friend right here."

—*His father,* whenever Matt and his brother Mark would fight as young boys

The weak can never forgive. Forgiveness is the attribute of the strong."

—*Mahatma Gandhi,* Indian nationalist leader, pioneer of non-violent civil disobedience

ANDRE AGASSI PROFESSIONAL TENNIS PLAYER, RANKED FIRST IN THE WORLD

 We must be careful in our decisions, careful in our words, and we must be careful in our relationships. Andre, we must live our life carefully."

—*Nelson Mandela,* President of South Africa, activist

MORGAN SPURLOCK DOCUMENTARY FILMMAKER, PRODUCER, SCREENWRITER, ACTIVIST

Son, there's three sides to every story. There's your story, there's my story, and there's the real story."

—*Ben Spurlock,* his father

Live Mindfully, Live Peacefully

Live simply so others may simply live."

—*Mother Teresa,* beatified Roman Catholic nun, founder of Missionaries of Charity, winner of the Nobel Peace Prize

ALBERT SCHWEITZER THEOLOGIAN, PHILOSOPHER, PHYSICIAN, MEDICAL MISSIONARY, NOBEL PEACE PRIZE WINNER

 If it be possible, as much as lieth in you, live peaceably with all men."

—*Romans 12:18*

FRANCIS BACON PHILOSOPHER, STATESMAN, SCIENTIST, AUTHOR

 It is the glory of a man to pass by an offense."

—*Proverbs 19:11*

We will walk the path not of retribution or revenge but the path of reconciliation and forgiveness."

—*Mahatma Gandhi,* Indian nationalist leader, pioneer of non-violent civil disobedience

When instead of reacting against a situation, you merge with it, the solution arises out of the situation itself."

—*Eckhart Tolle,* author

RON HOWARD ACTOR, PRODUCER, DIRECTOR, ON HIS
CO-STAR'S HARD WORK AND PERSISTENT GRACIOUSNESS TO HIS
AUDIENCE

 I appreciate it and
good night."

—*Andy Griffith,* actor, to audiences after his
shows

DOUGLAS MACARTHUR UNITED STATES GENERAL, CHIEF OF
STAFF OF THE UNITED STATES ARMY

 Old soldiers never die; they only fade away."

—*Song*

You know what I really need? . . . Absolutely nothing. I don't need a thing in the world. I am the happiest man on the face of the earth."

—*Father Mychal Judge,* Franciscan priest, first certified fatality of the 9/11 attacks

QUEEN NOOR OF JORDAN DOWAGER QUEEN OF JORDAN, ANTI-NUCLEAR WEAPONS ADVOCATE

 It should never be forgotten that peace resides ultimately not in the hands of governments, but in the hands of the people."

—*Hussein I,* King of Jordan, her late husband

MOTHER TERESA BEATIFIED ROMAN CATHOLIC NUN, FOUNDER OF MISSIONARIES OF CHARITY, WINNER OF THE NOBEL PEACE PRIZE

 My peace I leave with you, my peace I give unto you."

—*John 14:27*

WILLIAM URY CO-FOUNDER OF HARVARD UNIVERSITY'S PROGRAM ON NEGOTIATION, SENIOR FELLOW OF THE HARVARD NEGOTIATION PROJECT, AUTHOR, ADVISOR, MEDIATOR

 # When spiderwebs unite, they can halt even the lion."

—African proverb

ELIZABETH LESSER CO-FOUNDER OF THE OMEGA INSTITUTE, AUTHOR

 Our separation from each other is an optical illusion of consciousness."

—*Albert Einstein,* physicist

You know, we have a long road to go to finally get democracy in my country. But I don't believe in hope without endeavor. I don't believe in the hope of change, unless we take action to make it so."

—*Aung San Suu Kyi,* Chairperson and General Secretary of Myanmar's National League of Democracy, Nobel Peace Prize winner

Believe in Yourself

We must have perseverance and above all confidence in ourselves. We must believe that we are gifted for something and that this thing must be attained."

—*Marie Curie,* physicist, chemist, Nobel Prize winner in physics

This is really great. You should enjoy it."

—*Stephen King,* after reading Gaiman's comic *Sandman* and *Good Omens,* a novel co-authored with Terry Pratchett; cited by Gaiman "as the best advice [he's] ever been given"

Because the soul is progressive, it never quite repeats itself, but in every act attempts the production of a new and fairer whole."

—*Ralph Waldo Emerson,* essayist, lecturer, poet

May today there be peace within.

May you trust God that you are exactly where you are meant to be.

May you not forget the infinite possibilities that are born of faith.

May you use those gifts that you have received, and pass on the love that has been given to you.

May you be content knowing you are a child of God. Let this presence settle into your bones, and allow your soul the freedom to sing, dance, praise and love. It is there for each and every one of us."

—*Thérèse de Lisieux,* Catholic saint

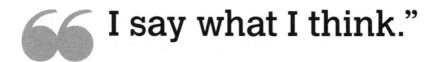

I say what I think."

—*Remy de Gourmont,* poet, novelist, critic

For the first time I examined myself with a seriously practical purpose. And there I found what appalled me: a zoo of lusts, a bedlam of ambitions, a nursery of fears, a harem of fondled hatreds."

—*C. S. Lewis,* author

KATHRYN SCHULZ JOURNALIST, AUTHOR

"I err therefore I am."

—*St. Augustine,* philosopher, theologian

I'll move to the White House, do the best I can, and if they don't like it, they can kick me out, but they can't make me be somebody I'm not."

—*Betty Ford,* First Lady of the United States

LIZ SMITH GOSSIP COLUMNIST

66 It is life as it is lived."

—*Gore Vidal,* author

The purpose of life is to be happy."

—*14th Dalai Lama,* head teacher of the Gelug tradition of Tibetan Buddhism, winner of the Nobel Peace Prize

I've never been a loser, and I'm not about to start now."

—*Vince Lombardi,* head coach of the Green Bay Packers

LARRY GELBART TELEVISON WRITER, PLAYWRIGHT, SCREENWRITER, AUTHOR

 There will be no limit for me in a few years, and I assure you that, by 1943, you will have the best answer in the world to anyone who thinks your son is crazy today—an answer in lights."

—*Gregory Peck,* actor, in a letter to his father; his film career took off in 1944

CAROLINE CASEY SOCIAL ENTREPRENEUR, CEO OF KANCHI, ACTIVIST FOR PEOPLE WITH DISABILITIES

 Be you."

—An unnamed friend

M, anything is possible. Just tell me what it is you want to achieve."

—*Guy Oseary,* her manager

Let's go do a great big Broadway show."

—*Lisa Banes,* actress, just before every stage performance of *The Philadelphia Story* in which they starred together

SIR BEN KINGSLEY ACTOR

 Give me a place to stand and I'll move the world."

—*Archimedes,* philospher

JOHN KRASINSKI ACTOR

 Well, you're just a funny guy."

—*B. J. Novak,* actor, producer, writer, and Krasinski's *Office* co-star and friend, upon casting Krasinski in his first on-stage role when they were in high school

Index